Editor
Sara Connolly

Managing Editor
Ina Massler Levin, M.A.

Illustrator
Sue Fullam

Cover Artist
Brenda DiAntonis

Art Manager
Kevin Barnes

Imaging
Craig Gunnell
James Edward Grace

Publisher
Mary D. Smith, M.S. Ed.

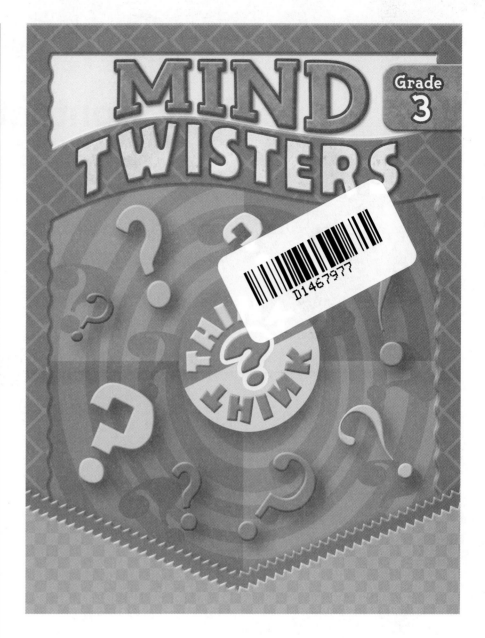

Author

Melissa Hart, M.F.A.

Teacher Created Resources, Inc.
6421 Industry Way
Westminster, CA 92683
www.teachercreated.com
ISBN-1-4206-3983-8
©2005 Teacher Created Resources, Inc.
Made in U.S.A.

Table of Contents

Table of Contents *(cont.)*

Introduction

Students learn well when both engaged and entertained. Brain teasers such as those found in *Mind Twisters* provide practice in valuable skills while keeping third grade students interested puzzles, word and math problems, riddles, and mazes.

The mind twisters can be used to start off the day, or they can be used to enrich the different areas of your curriculum. All of the mind twisters are leveled to be completed by individual learners, although you may choose to pair your students with a partner, if necessary.

In *Mind Twisters*, exercises have been organized into categories to supplement your regular educational curriculum. Each activity provides opportunities for further research in applicable subjects including language arts, mathematics, history, geography, science, and physical education.

Language Arts activities give students practice in identifying synonyms, idioms, and word construction. They are asked to rhyme words, solve rebus mysteries, and identify analogies.

A wide variety of critical thinking exercises in *Mind Twisters* will challenge students to solve interesting riddles, equations, and picture problems. **Mathematics** activities provide students with further practice in solving equations and working out answers to word problems.

Activities in **History** provide students with opportunities to study famous people and places. Geography pages ask students to consider fascinating geographical features. Science activities inspire students to consider inventions, branches of science, and animal classification.

The book concludes with activities related to **Physical Education**, followed by a comprehensive answer key to each exercise in *Mind Twisters*.

Incredible Idioms

Idioms are expressions used frequently within a language or culture. For instance, "He swept her off her feet" is one popular idiom. Study each picture below, and then write the appropriate idiom in the space beside it. The first one has been done for you.

1. _Cat got your tongue?_ _____

2. _____

3. _____

4. _____

5. _____

6. _____

Incredible Idioms II

Idioms are expressions used frequently within a language or culture. For instance, "He swept her off her feet" is one popular idiom. Study each picture below, and then write the appropriate idiom in the space beside it. The first one has been done for you.

1.   Look at the big picture.

2.

3.

4.

5.

6.

Incredible Idioms III

Idioms are expressions used frequently within a language or culture. For instance, "He swept her off her feet" is one popular idiom. Study each picture below, and then write the appropriate idiom in the space beside it. The first one has been done for you.

1. *Don't count your chickens before they're hatched.*

2. _____

3. _____

4. _____

5. _____

6. _____

Palindrome Play

A *palindrome* is a word which reads the same backwards or forwards, such as "wow". Answer each question or statement with a palindrome. The first one has been done for you.

1. What is another word for a child? _tot_

2. You use this to see. _____

3. She's your female parent. _____

4. What is the middle of the day? _____

5. You find her in a church. _____

6. This is the sound of a balloon breaking. _____

8

Palindrome Play II

A *palindrome* is a word which reads the same backwards or forwards. Answer each question or statement with a palindrome. The first one has been done for you.

1. This is a polite name for a woman. <u>Ma'am</u>

2. This is another name for your father. _____

3. These are what singers perform. _____

4. This is an exclamation. _____

5. This is the past tense of "do." _____

6. This is a short name for a baby dog. _____

Palindrome Play III

A *palindrome* is a word which reads the same backwards or forwards. Answer each question or statement with a palindrome. The first one has been done for you.

1. This is another word for energy. _____ pep _____

2. This is another word for a show. _____

3. This keeps a baby clean. _____

4. This is another word for a joke. _____

5. You can cross a river in this. _____

6. This is a nickname for Robert. _____

Analogies Are Awesome!

Find the relationship between the first pair for a clue on how to solve the second pair. The first one has been done for you.

1. Joey is to kangaroo as <u>lamb</u> is to sheep.

   Relationship: This is a baby animal and an adult animal.

2. Chapters are to books as songs are to _____.

   Relationship: _____

3. Peel is to orange as _____ is to muscles and bones.

   Relationship: _____

4. Notes are to music as _____ are to a daisy.

   Relationship: _____

5. Chill is to refrigerator as _____ is to oven.

   Relationship: _____

6. Lettuce is to salad as _____ are to spaghetti.

   Relationship: _____

Analogies Are Awesome! II

Find the relationship between the first pair for a clue on how to solve the second pair. The first one has been done for you.

1. Clown is to entertain as <u>doctor</u> is to heal.

   Relationship: These are employees and their jobs.

2. Shoe is to foot as hat is to _____

   Relationship: _____

3. Dollar bills are to wallet as _____ are to piggy bank.

   Relationship: _____

4. Hand is to baseball as _____ is to soccer.

   Relationship: _____

5. Fur is to cat as _____ are to snake.

   Relationship: _____

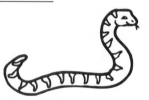

6. Tire is to bicycle as _____ is to inline skates.

   Relationship: _____

Analogies Are Awesome! III

Find the relationship between the first pair for a clue on how to solve the second pair. The first one has been done for you.

1. Sand is to a beach as <u>puzzle piece</u> is to a jigsaw puzzle.

   Relationship: These parts make up a whole.

2. Number is to clock as _____ is to tree.

   Relationship: _____

3. Hairbrush is to hair as _____ is to teeth.

   Relationship: _____

4. Hose is to firefighter as _____ is to gardener.

   Relationship: _____

5. Pen is to author as _____ is to artist.

   Relationship: _____

6. Stage is to actor as _____ is to swimmer.

   Relationship: _____

Word Ladders

Transform one word into another by changing one letter on each rung of the ladder. Each rung must be a valid word. Use the clues to help you.

The first one is done for you.

1. Change **MILK** into **PILL**

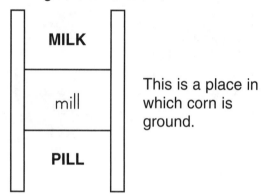

MILK

mill

PILL

This is a place in which corn is ground.

2. Change **HAND** into **BOND**

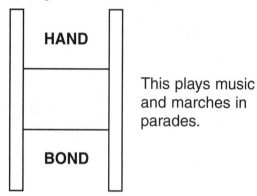

HAND

BOND

This plays music and marches in parades.

3. Change **ARMY** into **AIMS**

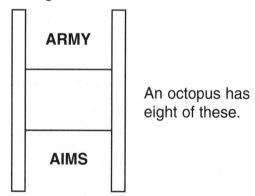

ARMY

AIMS

An octopus has eight of these.

4. Change **EASY** into **CANE**

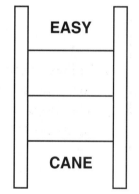

EASY

CANE

a. This means "without difficulty."
b. This is a container.

Word Ladders II

Transform one word into another by changing one letter in each rung of the ladder. Each link must be a valid word.

The first one is done for you.

1. Change **MICE** into **MATS**

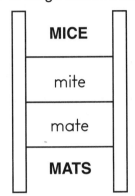

MICE

mite

mate

MATS

a. This is a tiny bug.

b. This is what you call your friend.

2. Change **CROOK** into **CLOWN**

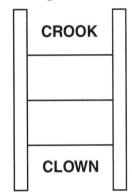

CROOK

CLOWN

a. This means to sing.

b. This is what you put on a king.

3. Change **MOON** into **MOLE**

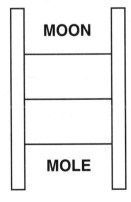

MOON

MOLE

a. This is another word for "dawn."

b. This is the opposite of less.

4. Change **COINS** into **CONES**

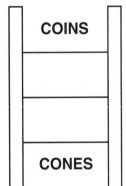

COINS

CONES

a. These are painful bumps on one's feet.

b. These are apple discards.

Word Ladders III

Transform one word into another by changing one letter on each rung of the ladder. Each link must be a valid word.

The first one is done for you.

1. Change **BLEED** into **DREAD**

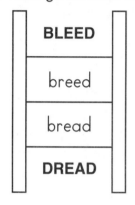

a. This means "a "type of animal.

b. This is used to make a sandwich.

2. Change **FLOUR** into **BLOOD**

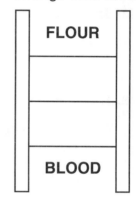

a. You might slip on this freshly-waxed surface.

b. This is sometimes the effect of too much rain.

3. Change **CLAP** into **SWAY**

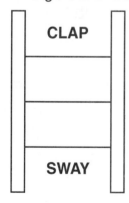

a. This is what you do to a mosquito.

b. This is another word for "barter."

4. Change **MORN** into **MALE**

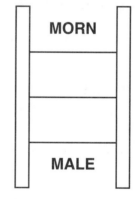

a. Many kids want this when it comes to dessert.

b. This is a furry rodent.

The Radical Rebus

A rebus is a picture which represents a word or phrase. Study each rebus below. Write down the word or phrase it symbolizes. The first one has been done for you.

1.

Red Riding Hood

Little Red Riding Hood

_____

2.

Bark

_____

_____

3.

cry
spilt milk

_____

_____

4.

rain
my parade

_____

_____

5.

PAwalkRK

_____

_____

6.

hCATat

_____

_____

The Radical Rebus II

A rebus is a picture which represents a word or phrase. Study each rebus below. Write down the word or phrase it symbolizes. The first one has been done for you.

1.

head
heels

head over heels

_____

2.

u deserve

a  today

_____

_____

3.

BADwolf

_____

_____

4.

Over

_____

_____

5.

feeling
world

_____

_____

6.

c   c
  o   o
    u   u
      n
    t   t
  r   r
y   y

_____

_____

The Radical Rebus III

A rebus is a picture which represents a word or phrase. Study each rebus below. Write down the word or phrase it symbolizes. The first one has been done for you.

1.

> walk
> H₂O

walk on water

_____

2.

> eggs eggs
> easy

_____

_____

3.

> cof_____fee

_____

_____

4.

> SHAVE

_____

_____

5.

> s
> l
> o
> w

_____

_____

6.

> who's
> first

_____

_____

Riddles that Rhyme

Answer these riddles with two words that rhyme. The first one has been done for you.

1. a thief in a library: _____ a book crook _____

2. navy-colored slime: _____

3. a purple monkey: _____

4. a ten-cent green fruit: _____

5. a plump rodent: _____

6. a terrific film: _____

Riddles that Rhyme II

Answer these riddles with two words that rhyme. The first one has been done for you.

1. a class guideline: _____ a school rule _____

2. a cheerful father: _____

3. an idle flower: _____

4. a female horse's mane: _____

5. a false reptile: _____

6. a quiet mother: _____

Riddles that Rhyme III

Answer these riddles with two words that rhyme. The first one has been done for you.

1. a toad race: _____ frog jog _____

2. a silly rabbit: _____

3. a tiny oak: _____

4. insect love: _____

5. a glass of pen juice: _____

6. a robin's speech: _____

22

Parts of Speech Word Search

Find the parts of speech from the Word Bank in the word search below. They are across, down, diagonal, and sometimes backwards!

```
D   U   W   E   K   Z   J   H   N   A   H   G
O   U   P   U   V   P   N   O   F   G   R   U
M   Q   Y   T   L   K   U   W   M   B   M   H
T   A   N   Q   M   N   P   O   L   L   S   A
P   R   B   Z   F   B   M   H   O   F   S   D
W   R   O   O   B   X   K   D   Z   L   F   V
Q   X   O   A   D   J   E   C   T   I   V   E
K   J   S   N   P   W   K   B   R   E   V   R
J   M   Y   F   O   W   J   N   G   R   J   B
K   D   T   G   T   U   M   A   T   Q   A   E
H   B   U   T   Z   A   N   Z   G   U   Y   K
T   P   R   E   P   O   S   I   T   I   O   N
```

ADJECTIVE	NOUN	VERB
ADVERB	PRONOUN	PREPOSITION

Family Plates

A car license plate can tell something about its owner. Which driver is a mother? Which is a grandfather? Decode the license plates below to find out who owns which car. The first one has been done for you.

1. **HER*BRO**　　　　　brother

2. **ANTNCAR**　　　　　_____

3. **ILUVMOM**　　　　　_____

4. **UNCLAMI**　　　　　_____

5. **IGRANNY**　　　　　_____

6. **IAMPAPA**　　　　　_____

An Amazing Equation

Follow the instructions below to work out this remarkable math equation. Be sure to complete the instructions in order. You may need a piece of scratch paper in order to work some equations.

1. Write down the number of the month you were born. _____
   (For instance, if you were born in April, write down 4 .

2. Multiply the number above by 4.

   _____ x 4 = _____

3. Add 13 to the number above.

   _____ + 13 = _____

4. Multiply the number above by 25.

   _____ x 25 = _____

5. Subtract 200 from the number above.

   _____ – 200 = _____

6. Add the day of the month on which you were born to the number above.

   _____ + _____ = _____

7. Multiply the number above by 2.

   _____ x 2 = _____

8. Subtract 40 from the number above.

   _____ – 40 = _____

9. Multiply the number above by 50.

   _____ x 50 = _____

10. Add the last two digits of the year of your birth to the number above.

    _____ + _____ = _____

11. Subtract 10,500 from the number above.

    _____ – 10,500 = _____

What's amazing about your answer?

_____

Number Square

Arrange the numbers 1 to 9 in the blocks, placing one number in each block, so that when you add the numbers in any column, horizontally or vertically, the sum must equal 15.

Adding up Animal Facts

Discover some facts about animals by solving the code below. First, answer each multiplication problem. Then, complete the puzzle below.

3 x 4732 = _____ A	8 x 2348 = _____ N	7356 x 4 = _____ T
3271 x 7 = _____ E	9 x 4321 = _____ Y	8 x 6573 = _____ D
6 x 3821 = _____ H	1 x 9843 = _____ P	9485 x 3 = _____ X
5943 x 3 = _____ M	3243 x 8 = _____ B	9 x 3756 = _____ O
7958 x 5 = _____ R	9 x 4635 = _____ C	3265 x 5 = _____ K
7 x 3251 = _____ L	5967 x 3 = _____ Z	8354 x 6 = _____ S
9321 x 2 = _____ G	2 x 8432 = _____ F	8 x 6847 = _____ I
9854 x 4 = _____ W	3 x 9867 = _____ J	

1. This bird has lopsided ears and telescopic vision.

   _____   _____   _____
   33,804   39,416   22,757

2. These mammals have a thumb and four fingers, just like humans.

   _____   _____   _____   _____
   25,944   14,196   29,424   50,124

3. This animal is the largest member of the canine family.

   _____   _____   _____   _____
   39,416   33,804   22,757   16,864

4. This animal has large paws that act like snowshoes in deep snow.

   _____   _____   _____   _____
   22,757   38,889   18,784   28,455

5. These water animals have a complex form of communication.

   _____   _____   _____   _____   _____   _____
   39,416   22,926   14,196   22,757   22,897   50,124

Adding Up Environmental Facts

Discover some facts about recycling by solving the code below. First, answer each division problem. Then, complete the puzzle below.

144 ÷ 12 = _____ A	63 ÷ 3 = _____ J	100 ÷ 5 = _____ S
16 ÷ 4 = _____ B	70 ÷ 7 = _____ K	154 ÷ 11 = _____ T
40 ÷ 5 = _____ C	95 ÷ 5 = _____ L	100 ÷ 4 = _____ U
12 ÷ 4 = _____ D	4 ÷ 4 = _____ M	72 ÷ 3 = _____ V
56 ÷ 8 = _____ E	90 ÷ 5 = _____ N	92 ÷ 4 = _____ W
36 ÷ 6 = _____ F	84 ÷ 4 = _____ O	132 ÷ 6 = _____ X
22 ÷ 2 = _____ G	58 ÷ 2 = _____ P	140 ÷ 5 = _____ Y
35 ÷ 7 = _____ H	64 ÷ 4 = _____ Q	93 ÷ 3 = _____ Z
24 ÷ 12 = _____ I	65 ÷ 5 = _____ R	

1. This can be recycled into carpeting and clothes.

___ ___ ___ ___ ___ ___ ___
29 19 12 20 14 2   8

2. Instead of throwing this away, grow it into an attractive plant.

___ ___ ___ ___ ___ ___
29 21 14 12 14 21

3. Recycling a soda can saves enough energy to run this for three hours.

___ ___
14 24

4. You can save water by taking this type of shower.

___ ___ ___ ___ ___
20 5   21 13 14

5. This can waste 25–30 gallons of water a day!

___ ___ ___ ___
19 7   12 10

6. You can use this to wrap presents!

___ ___ ___ ___ ___ ___ ___ ___ ___
18 7   23 20 29 12 29 7   13

Adding up Facts about Famous Authors

Discover some facts about authors by solving the code below. First, answer each fraction problem. Then, complete the puzzle below.

$\frac{1}{8} + \frac{4}{8} =$ _____ D $\qquad$ $\frac{3}{5} - \frac{2}{5} =$ _____ I $\qquad$ $\frac{5}{8} + \frac{2}{8} =$ _____ C

$\frac{2}{6} + \frac{4}{6} =$ _____ R $\qquad$ $\frac{4}{15} + \frac{3}{15} =$ _____ K $\qquad$ $\frac{7}{10} - \frac{4}{10} =$ _____ T

$\frac{1}{5} + \frac{2}{5} =$ _____ W $\qquad$ $\frac{2}{7} - \frac{0}{7} =$ _____ Y $\qquad$ $\frac{1}{6} + \frac{4}{6} =$ _____ U

$\frac{2}{2} - \frac{1}{2} =$ _____ A $\qquad$ $\frac{3}{9} + \frac{4}{9} =$ _____ L $\qquad$ $\frac{5}{7} - \frac{3}{7} =$ _____ J

$\frac{1}{3} - \frac{0}{3} =$ _____ N $\qquad$ $\frac{4}{7} - \frac{3}{7} =$ _____ M $\qquad$ $\frac{1}{2} + \frac{5}{2} =$ _____ V

$\frac{4}{6} - \frac{3}{6} =$ _____ F $\qquad$ $\frac{8}{9} - \frac{4}{9} =$ _____ B $\qquad$ $\frac{6}{3} + \frac{6}{3} =$ _____ E

$\frac{5}{5} - \frac{3}{5} =$ _____ G $\qquad$ $\frac{4}{5} + \frac{0}{5} =$ _____ O

$\frac{8}{3} - \frac{6}{3} =$ _____ H $\qquad$ $\frac{1}{4} - \frac{1}{4} =$ _____ P

1. You can visit Orchard House in Massachusetts, where Louisa May Alcott wrote this novel.

   ___ ___ ___ ___ ___ ___   ___ ___ ___ ___ ___
   $\frac{7}{9}$ $\frac{1}{5}$ $\frac{3}{10}$ $\frac{3}{10}$ $\frac{7}{9}$ 4 $\frac{3}{5}$ $\frac{4}{5}$ $\frac{1}{7}$ 4 $\frac{1}{3}$

2. She wrote this in between her infant daughter's naps.

   ___ ___ ___ ___ ___ ___ ___ ___ ___ ___ ___
   $\frac{2}{3}$ $\frac{1}{2}$ 1 1 $\frac{2}{7}$ 0 $\frac{4}{5}$ $\frac{3}{10}$ $\frac{3}{10}$ 4 1

3. This author of *The Call of the Wild* sailed on a sealing ship.

   ___ ___ ___ ___ ___ ___ ___ ___ ___ ___
   $\frac{2}{7}$ $\frac{1}{2}$ $\frac{7}{8}$ $\frac{7}{15}$ $\frac{7}{9}$ $\frac{4}{5}$ $\frac{1}{3}$ $\frac{5}{8}$ 45 $\frac{1}{3}$

4. Roald Dahl, author of *James and the Giant Peach*, kept this a secret from the time he was eight years old.

   ___ ___ ___ ___ ___
   $\frac{5}{8}$ $\frac{1}{5}$ $\frac{1}{2}$ 1 $\frac{2}{7}$

5. The author of *Hatchet*, Gary Paulsen, ran away from home at age fourteen and joined this.

   ___ ___ ___ ___ ___ ___ ___ ___
   $\frac{7}{8}$ $\frac{1}{2}$ 1 $\frac{1}{3}$ $\frac{1}{5}$ 3 $\frac{1}{2}$ $\frac{7}{9}$

Geometry Mind Twister

Write one number, 1 through 8, in each square, so that squares with consecutive numbers (that is, 1, 2, 3, or 4, 5, 6 for example) do not touch.

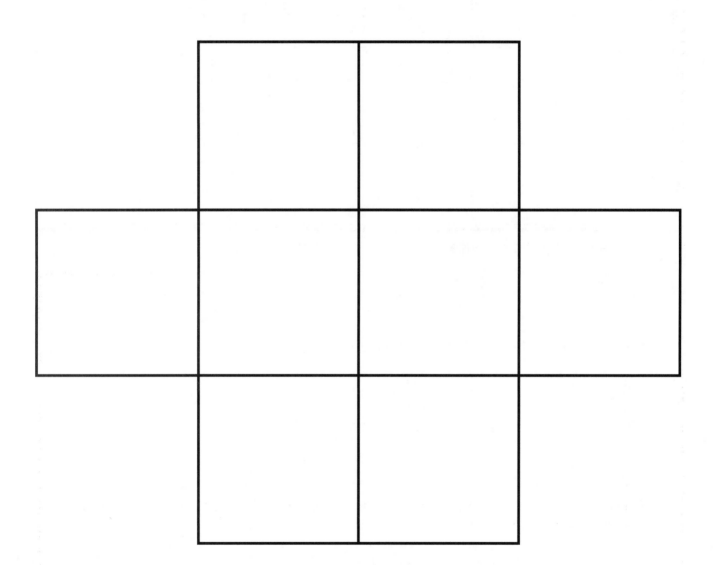

Geometry Mind Twister II

Divide this shape into four identical parts.

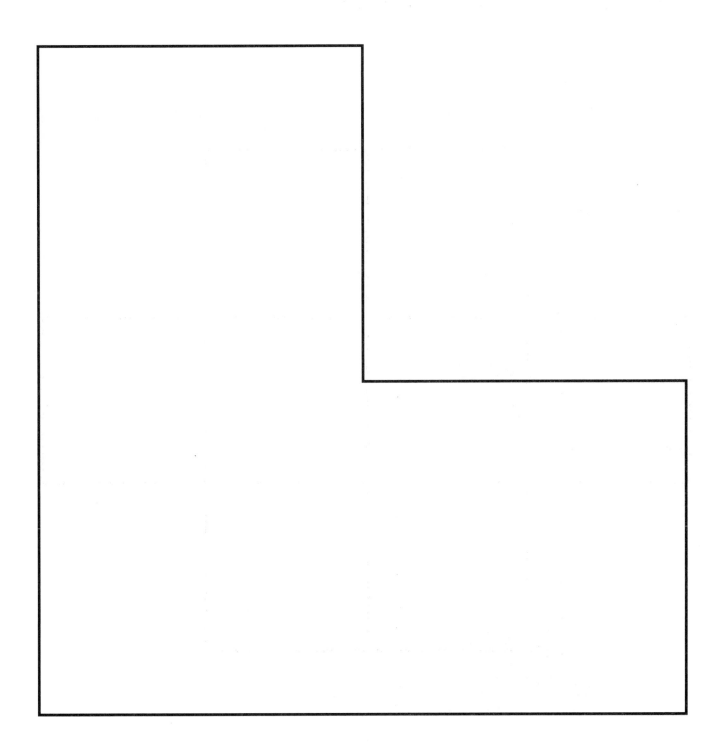

Rat Math

Six third-graders have pet rats. On Valentine's Day, Whitey was two years old. Templeton is two months older than Whitey. Pinky is six months younger than Templeton. When Sam and Annie were born in the same litter, Pinky was three months old. Fluffy is six months older than Sam and Annie. Tiny is two months younger than the two litter mates.

In what month was each rat born?

Month	Rat's Name
January	
February	
March	
April	
May	
June	
July	
August	
September	
October	
November	
December	

Math Word Search

Find the math words from the word bank below in this word search. They are across, down, diagonal, and sometimes backwards!

```
R  N  T  H  Z  D  C  Q  Y  E  A  E  I  R
B  S  C  Y  H  W  E  L  N  V  S  T  W  F
R  R  A  U  P  H  P  C  S  E  F  K  R  R
V  I  R  X  E  I  S  T  I  R  G  Z  D  A
E  A  T  Y  T  N  O  G  C  M  M  P  I  T
A  T  B  L  W  U  P  F  E  B  A  P  V  C
D  R  U  M  R  E  O  G  I  Z  Y  L  I  A
Q  M  S  F  R  A  C  T  I  O  N  S  D  K
Z  W  E  O  Z  T  F  T  U  H  Y  D  E  N
S  D  Y  I  B  V  R  U  Y  T  N  W  F  V
V  M  U  X  K  M  C  G  Y  O  Y  Y  H  N
M  F  D  D  K  L  T  R  P  O  N  F  U  X
U  T  R  D  Y  Z  Z  I  B  Z  I  N  F  K
O  L  Q  S  E  L  S  U  G  N  L  T  G  E
```

Word Bank

ADD	DIVIDE	MULTIPLY
DECIMAL	FRACTION	SUBTRACT

Famous Duos

See if you can name the missing partner in each of the famous pairs from books, television, movies, and history. The first one has been done for you.

1. Lady and ___The Tramp_____. (movie)

2. Bert and _____ (TV)

3. Mickey Mouse and _____ (TV)

4. Beauty and the _____ (Book/movie)

5. Jack and _____ (nursery rhyme)

6. The Tortoise and the _____ (fable)

Famous Trios

See if you can name these famous trios from books, television, movies, and history. The first one has been done for you.

1. They entertained viewers with TV comedy.

   The Three Stooges
   _____

2. A little girl ate their porridge and slept in their beds.

   _____

3. They built houses made of straw, wood, and brick.

   _____

4. They lost their tails to the farmer's wife.

   _____

5. They are boats which carried Columbus to America.

   _____

6. They're Donald Duck's nephews in Disney cartoons.

   _____

Scrambled Presidents

Unscramble the following words to reveal the first names of former presidents of the United States. The first one has been done for you.

1. sJeam **Polk**   James Polk

2. drAwen **Jackson**   _____

3. Mtrain **van Buren**   _____

4. aharbmA **Lincoln**   _____

5. mymiJ **Carter**   _____

6. limWali **Clinton**   _____

Scrambled Women in History

Unscramble the following words to reveal the first names of women who have made history in the U.S.. The first one has been done for you.

1. loDly **Madison**: This former first lady saved a portrait of George Washington from a fire.

   Dolly Madison

2. soRa **Parks**: She helped to inspire the Civil Rights movement.

   _____

3. yaMa **Lin**: She is the artist/architect who designed the Vietnam Veterans Memorial.

   _____

4. riraetH **Tubman**: She was famous for helping to free the slaves.

   _____

5. ymlEi **Dickinson**: She is a famous poet from the 19th century.

   _____

6. hairstC **Mcauliffe**: She was chosen to be the first teacher in space.

   _____

Scrambled Geography

Unscramble the geographical features below. The first one has been done for you.

1. tresed   _desert_ _____

2. kale   _____

3. inuntamo   _____

4. laveyl   _____

4. lihl   _____

5. onace   _____

6. verir   _____

Geography Fill-In

Read each description, then fill in the correct word. The first one has been done for you.

1. This is a large block of ice. g l a c i e r .

2. This can erupt with lava. _____ _____ l _____ _____ n _____

3. This is covered in sand. _____ _____ s _____ _____ t

4. This land is surrounded by water. _____ _____ l _____ n _____

5. This is a small river. _____ t _____ _____ _____ m

6. This is fast-falling water. _____ _____ t _____ _____ f _____ l _____

How Many Went Where?

Four groups of pioneers traveled from Wisconsin to Oregon. Some men went on horseback. A family traveled in a covered wagon. Some newlyweds also traveled in a wagon. One family went on horseback.

Using the clues below, discover how many people were in each group, how they traveled, and the order in which they arrived in Oregon.

- The two men, who arrived first, didn't have protection from the rain.

- The two newlywed couples arrived last.

- A family of four rode two stallions and two mares behind the other group on horseback.

- The two newlywed couples followed the couple who traveled with three children.

How Many People	How They Traveled	Order in Which They Arrived

A Picture Worth 1000 Words

Study each picture below to decode a word or phrase relating to U.S. history. The first one has been done for you.

1.   **WHITE**   **+**   🏠   **=**   White House

2.      **+**   🦅   **=** _____

3.    **of LIB +** **+** 🫖 **− pot =** _____

4.   ☆☆☆ **and** 👕 **4 + ever =** _____

5.   **You're a** **−ma+old+** 🇺🇸 **=** _____

6.    **+** 🌳 **+ ot =** _____

Historical Rhyming Riddles

The following riddles can be answered with two words that rhyme. The underlined word in the riddle should be used in the answer.

1. a lawful <u>eagle</u>: _____ a legal eagle _____

2. an independent <u>me</u>: _____

3. a man who draws a U.S. <u>map</u>: _____

4. a <u>flaw</u> in a rule: _____

5. a sack for the <u>flag</u>: _____

6. a confusing <u>history</u>: _____

American Slang

Slang refers to speech used in a playful manner. Match the phrases on the left with the slang on the right. The first one is done for you.

1. My stomach is full.

2. He's angry.

3. Goodbye!

4. I have no money.

5. I promise.

6. I made a mistake.

a. Cross my heart.

b. I made a boo-boo.

c. I'm stuffed.

d. He's flipped his lid.

e. Ta ta!

f. I'm broke.

American Slang II

Slang refers to speech used in a playful manner. Match the phrases on the left with the slang on the right. The first one is done for you.

1. Stop what you're doing.

2. Give me a dollar.

3. I'm sitting in the sun.

4. That's terrific.

5. He's lazy.

6. That's disgusting.

a. I'm catching some rays.

b. That's cool.

c. Give me a buck.

d. Break it up.

e. That's gross.

f. He's a couch potato.

American Slang III

Slang refers to speech used in a playful manner. Study the Slang Bank below. Then fill in the blanks with the correct slang phrase that matches the given phrase.

1. You'd say this to describe a girl with courage.

   _____

2. You'd say this to someone you like a lot.

   _____

3. You'd say this about a boy who's very calm.

   _____

4. You'd say this to someone who's causing trouble.

   _____

5. You'd say this to someone who's worrying.

   _____

6. You'd say this about an easy quiz.

   _____

Slang Bank

It's a piece of cake.

He's so laid-back.

She's got guts.

Don't sweat it.

I get a kick out of you.

Stop making waves.

Categories

Read the clues about parts of the body and fill in the category. The first one has been done for you.

1. George Washington, Abraham Lincoln, George Bush

   Category: ___U.S. Presidents___

2. Mary Todd Lincoln, Abigail Adams, Hilary Clinton

   Category: _____

3. U.S. Capitol, Lincoln Memorial, Washington Monument

   Category: _____

4. Bald eagle, American flag, Great Seal of the United States

   Category: _____

5. *America the Beautiful, My Country 'Tis of Thee, The Star-Spangled Banner*

   Category: _____

6. dime, dollar bill, penny

   Category: _____

Patriotic Word Search

Find the words from the Word Bank below in this word search. They are across, down, diagonal, and sometimes backwards!

```
L  S  K  X  F  X  E  V  C  N  S  C  T  I  F
C  L  T  Q  G  Y  P  L  I  B  E  R  T  Y  Y
B  P  E  R  Q  F  K  I  K  J  W  N  P  W  H
N  X  F  B  I  P  U  V  P  M  F  N  X  S  P
I  U  K  Q  B  P  I  T  E  W  W  P  V  A  H
E  E  R  F  R  V  E  S  A  L  T  J  D  N  S
C  E  R  T  V  U  X  S  G  J  J  L  K  N  B
E  C  D  L  L  G  W  B  L  Q  S  U  S  M  Y
Y  T  A  T  P  T  O  Y  E  Y  J  C  H  B  E
X  Y  R  I  G  H  T  S  P  H  I  V  S  V  C
P  U  Y  P  W  H  T  Q  U  T  A  T  D  O  I
V  F  Y  O  D  K  K  U  N  D  A  S  T  K  T
K  L  G  B  Z  I  G  A  W  R  S  Z  F  D  S
S  A  Z  A  Q  F  V  S  S  H  I  K  M  R  U
H  G  B  O  O  E  P  C  W  P  N  Q  K  W  J
```

BELL	FREE	RIGHTS	LIBERTY	STRIPES
EAGLE	FLAG	JUSTICE	STARS	

History Plates

Study each license plate for a clue to who its owner is. (Keep in mind that the car wasn't yet invented during the lifetime of some of these historical figures!) The first one is done for you.

1. **1STPREZ**   George Washington

2. **IMTEDDY**   _____

3. **ILUVABE**   _____

4. ***MLKJR**   _____

5. **ICARTER**   _____

6. **MY*FLAG**   _____

48

Teacher's Day

Teacher's Day is celebrated around the world on October fifth. Read the clues below about teachers and fill in the blanks. The first one has been done for you.

1. A teacher uses this to write.

   c h a l k

2. Teachers offer this to keep you learning after school.

   _____ o _____ _____ w _____ _____ k

3. What your teacher expects you do to in class each day.

   _____ e _____ r _____

4. People give this fruit to teachers.

   _____ p _____ _____ _____

5. These are a teacher's best friends.

   b _____ _____ _____ _____

6. What a teacher uses to show you the world.

   _____ l _____ b _____

Historical Transportation

Transportation has changed throughout history. Read the clues below about transportation and fill in the blanks. The first one has been done for you.

1. This changed transportation forever.

   <u>w</u> <u>h</u> <u>e</u> <u>e</u> <u>l</u>

2. The Vikings sailed in these.

   s ____ i ____ ____

3. Native Americans used these to cross large bodies of water.

   k ____ y ____ k ____

4. Orville and Wilbur Wright flew this at Kitty Hawk.

   ____ ____ r ____ l ____ n ____

5. Henry Ford built this in the early 1900s.

   ____ u ____ ____ m ____ b ____ ____ e

6. This moves people through their city together.

   ____ ____ s

U.S.A. Trivia

Figure out the answers to these trivia questions about the United States of America.

1. The first Flag Day in the United States was celebrated on June 14, 1777. How many years ago was this first celebration? _____

2. The U.S. flag had 13 stars in 1777. How many more stars does it have now?

   _____

3. On July 4, 1776, the United States declared itself free of British rule. How many years has the U.S. been a free country? _____

4. Frances Bellamy wrote The Pledge of Allegiance in 1892. How long ago was it written?

   _____

5. Francis Scott Key wrote the words to "The Star Spangled Banner" in 1814. This poem became the United States national anthem in 1931. How many years after it was written did this poem become the national anthem? _____

6. George Washington became the first United States president in 1789. How many years ago was he sworn in as the first U.S. president? _____

Amazing Maze

Help the bald eagle fly back to the Capitol Building.

Science Plates

Study each license plate for a clue to what its owner studies. The first one has been done for you.

1. **DR*BUGZ**   bugs

2. **LUVROCK**   _____

3. **DR*MEOW**   _____

4. **DIGBONZ**   _____

5. **LVBIRDS**   _____

6. **WOOFDOC**   _____

Categories

Read the clues about parts of the body and fill in the category.
The first one has been done for you.

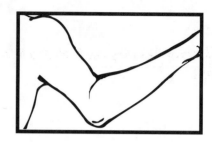

1. wrist, elbow, shoulder

   Category: _____ These are parts of the arm. _____

2. toe, ankle, heel

   Category: _____

3. ear, eye, nose

   Category: _____

4. tooth, tongue, gum

   Category: _____

5. eyelash, pupil, lid

   Category: _____

6. thigh, knee, shin

   Category: _____

Matching

Match the body part on the left to its function on the right. The first one has been done for you.

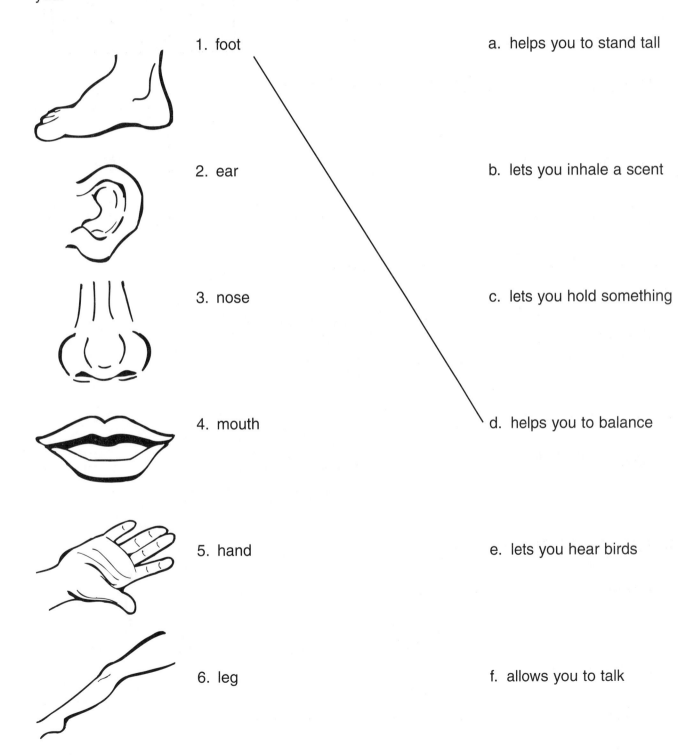

1. foot   a. helps you to stand tall

2. ear   b. lets you inhale a scent

3. nose   c. lets you hold something

4. mouth   d. helps you to balance

5. hand   e. lets you hear birds

6. leg   f. allows you to talk

Analogies

Finding the relationship between the objects in the first part of the analogies gives you the key to solving the second part. Choose the word that best completes each analogy below. The first one has been done for you.

1. Foot is to shoe as _____hand_____ is to glove.

2. Ring is to finger as _____ is to ear.

3. Toothbrush is to teeth as washcloth is to _____.

4. Knee is to leg as _____ is to arm.

5. Fingernail is to finger as _____ is to toe.

6. Jacket is to arms as _____ are to legs.

Connect the Dots

Without lifting your pencil from the page, draw no more than four straight lines to connect the dots below.

O   O   O

O   O   O

O   O   O

Scrambled Inventions

Unscramble the inventions below. The first one has been done for you.

1. heelw   _____ wheel _____

2. diroa   _____

3. ocklc   _____

4. veno   _____

5. kibec   _____

6. sitenoerli   _____

Scrambled Transportation Inventions

Unscramble the transportation inventions below. The first one has been done for you.

1. rac   _____car_____

2. rinta   _____

3. nepla   _____

4. toab   _____

5. tej   _____

6. takses   _____

Scrambled Scientific Inventions

Study the clues, then unscramble the scientific inventions below. The first one has been done for you.

1. borot _____robot_____ Clue: You can program this to complete tasks.

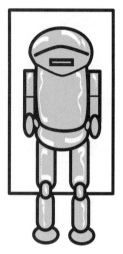

2. peelnothe _____ Clue: You can call on this.

3. raxy _____ Clue: This allows you to see inside.

4. tumropec _____ Clue: You can do research and type.

5. vimwearco _____ Clue: This allows you to cook quickly.

6. rcspoomice _____ Clue: This makes small things look big.

Planet Word Search

Find the planets from the Word Bank below in this word search. They are across, down, diagonal, and sometimes backwards!

```
M   W   P   E   Q   I   U   Z   H   N   G   C

V   A   R   E   T   I   P   U   J   S   L   B

F   A   R   N   L   O   M   F   C   U   I   E

N   K   S   S   R   H   P   G   J   N   X   B

C   G   I   S   Y   U   Q   T   D   E   N   P

N   F   U   U   V   X   T   Q   J   V   V   H

E   S   E   N   U   T   C   A   R   R   T   C

P   X   X   A   Q   N   C   O   S   R   P   L

T   I   S   R   G   I   W   G   A   O   W   H

U   P   L   U   T   O   F   E   V   U   V   I

N   E   G   M   A   U   I   S   L   O   L   L

E   X   F   U   K   M   E   R   C   U   R   Y
```

JUPITER	PLUTO	NEPTUNE
SATURN	EARTH	URANUS
MARS	VENUS	MERCURY

Gatherings of Birds

Did you know that a group of crows is called a "murder," and a group of turkeys is called a "rafter"? Study the picture clues below to discover the names of other groups of birds.

1. A _____ of pheasants

2. A _____ of nightingales

3. A _____ of swallows

4. A _____ of jays

5. A _____ of hawks

Gatherings of Animals

Did you know that a group of rhinoceros is called a "crash," and a group of mosquitoes is called a "scourge"? Study the picture clues below to discover the names of other groups of animals.

1. A _____ of salmon

2. A _____ of gorillas

3. A_____ of caterpillars

4. A _____ of clams

5. A _____ of fish

5. A_____ of leopards

Science Parade

The third grade science parade had students in costume—a group dressed as beetles, a group dressed as spiders, one dressed as ants, one as centipedes, and one group as frogs.

Read the description of each group and decide how many are in each group, and in what order they marched in the parade.

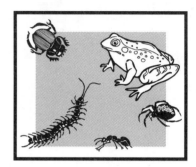

- The two centipedes were made up of five students each, and they marched behind the spiders.

- Only one student dressed as a frog.

- The ants marched in three groups of two, just ahead of the frog.

- Four beetles marched in front of the spiders.

- The centipedes followed three students dressed as spiders.

Position in Parade	Number of Students	Costume

A Circle of Pennies

Change two rows of pennies into a oval by moving only two pennies.
Hint: You might want to try this with real pennies.

Change:

To this:

But remember, only move two pennies!

Puzzling Pattern

Study the words below. Something is the same about all of them. Can you figure out what it is?

cabinet	oven	towel
tiger	rabid	later

_____

_____

_____

_____

66

Science Maze

Help the scientist find his way back to the laboratory.

Mysterious Numbers

Each of the clues below contains a number, words, and letters that symbolize commonly recognized phrases. Figure out each phrase. The first one has been done for you.

1. 9 Planets in the SS   9 Planets in the Solar System

2. 4 P on a cat   _____

3. 1 W on a unicycle   _____

4. 12 N on a clock   _____

5. 8 sides on a SS   _____

6. 8 L on a spider   _____

Mysterious Numbers II

Each of the clues below contains a number, words, and letters that symbolize commonly recognized phrases. Figure out each phrase. The first one has been done for you.

1. 5 T on a foot   _____5 toes on a foot_____

2. 7 C in the world   _____

3. 32 T in your mouth   _____

4. 7 days in a W   _____

5. 24 H in a D   _____

6. 10 F on your H   _____.

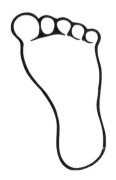

Sports Talk

People around the world play interesting sports. Using the clues below, fill in the blanks.

1. This is called football in England.

   _____ _____ _____ _____ _____ _____

2. This is a game played on horseback.

   _____ _____ _____ _____

3. In this game, players can steal.

   _____ _____ _____ _____ _____ _____ _____ _____

4. You need a saber for this sport.

   _____ _____ _____ _____ _____ _____ _____ _____

5. Competitors in this sport call the square a "ring."

   _____ _____ _____ _____ _____ _____

6. You compete in this sport with a pack of dogs.

   _____ _____ _____ _____ _____ _____ _____

More Sports Talk

Many sports require particular equipment. Using the clues below, fill in the blanks.

1. Baseball has four.

   _____ _____ _____ _____ _____

2. Hockey players need this.

   _____ _____ _____ _____

3. Football players must wear this.

   _____ _____ _____ _____ _____ _____

4. In tennis, each player has this.

   _____ _____ _____ _____ _____ _____

5. Croquet players need one.

   _____ _____ _____ _____ _____

6. In ping pong, there are two.

   _____ _____ _____ _____ _____ _____

Sports Categories

Read the clues about sports and fill in the category. The first one has been done for you.

1. paddle, oar, arm

   Category: _____ They move you across the water. _____

2. wheel, seat, chain

   Category: _____

3. field, rink, court

   Category: _____

4. kneepads, helmet, goggles

   Category: _____

5. horse, bicycle, go-cart

   Category: _____

6. skis, skates, cleats

   Category: _____

Sports Categories II

Read the clues about sports and fill in the category. The first one has been done for you.

1. Racket, bat, paddle

   Category: _____ These are items with which to hit a ball. _____

2. basketball, birdie, puck

   Category: _____

3. swimming pool, track, boxing ring

   Category: _____

4. bathing suit, running shorts, leotard

   Category: _____

5. snowshoes, ice skates, fins

   Category: _____

6. helmet, bathing cap, baseball cap

   Category: _____

Hiking Fun

A third-grade class completed a survey on where each student loved to hike. Their choices were:

in the mountains

on the beach

by a river

around a lake

Hiking Spots	Tally	Number
	~~IIII~~ ~~IIII~~ II	
	IIII	
	III	
	~~IIII~~	

The chart above shows the results of the survey, but doesn't include the names of the choices. Using the clues below, fill in the name of each hiking spot, and the total number of students who chose it.

Clues:

- The beach was chosen most.
- The mountains were chosen least.
- By a river was chosen more than around a lake.

Jersey Stripes

Your new bicycling jersey has stripes in a pattern: red, yellow, red, yellow, blue, red, yellow, blue, green. The pattern continues near the bottom with pink, orange, purple, and white stripes. How many stripes are on your colorful jersey?_____

Hint: Illustrate the pattern with colors or words, adding each new color as it appears.

Track Practice

Coach Smith asks his runners to practice a varying pattern of distance each afternoon. First, he asks runners to do 1/16 mile run and 1/8 mile jog, then 1/8 mile run and 1/4 mile jog, then 1/4 mile run and 1/2 mile jog, and so on. Can you predict the last two running and jogging distances based on this pattern?

76

Sports Search

Find the sports words from the Word Bank below in this word search. They are across, down, diagonal, and sometimes backwards!

```
R  V  G  E  S  E  Y  R  B  H  Z  X  K
V  V  F  P  L  E  T  U  U  F  V  B  G
C  Q  O  X  K  V  R  U  M  G  Q  T  B
T  S  A  C  U  D  A  G  C  P  B  P  R
Z  Z  O  Z  U  Z  C  Z  O  Z  V  Y  Z
U  H  J  V  Y  K  K  L  J  I  H  G  L
F  J  A  H  V  E  O  U  X  O  U  N  W
B  E  W  H  E  X  Q  Z  A  Q  U  I  Z
E  C  Y  X  F  S  D  U  R  H  T  L  B
V  J  J  U  W  L  N  I  P  T  S  C  W
U  Y  W  P  M  L  S  Y  X  V  V  Y  D
B  O  X  I  N  G  D  H  O  V  O  C  R
M  F  E  O  V  J  M  S  K  O  B  R  T
```

HOCKEY	CYCLING	POLO
RUGBY	TRACK	BOXING

Double Letters in Sports

Answer each sports clue with a word that contains double letters. The first one has been done for you.

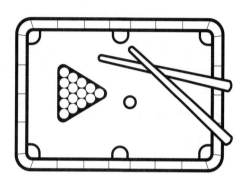

1. _____Pool_____ is a game played on a table with balls and cue sticks.

2. Basketball players try to throw a ball through a

_____.

3. "Swing, _____!" is a cry heard at baseball games.

4. Bicyclists need two _____ on their bikes.

5. When playing _____ your hands can't touch the ball.

6. Baseball players keep their eye on the

_____.

Double Letters in Sports II

Answer each sports clue with a word that contains double letters. The first one has been done for you.

1. Kayakers need a _____paddle_____ to move across the water.

2. Swimmers compete in a _____.

3. In _____, two players hit a ball across a net.

4. The only equipment _____ need is a pair of shoes.

5. Serious hikers need to carry water and _____.

6. _____ is a sport which requires snow.

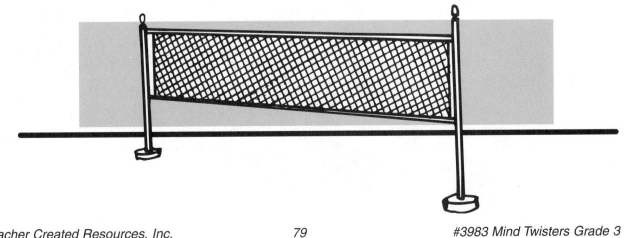

Double Letters in Sports III

Answer each sports clue with a word that contains double letters. The first one has been done for you.

1. Kayakers need a _____paddle_____ to move across the water.

2. Inline skaters need _____ and elbow pads to protect their bodies.

3. A racecar can't move without _____.

4. _____ requires two teams, a ball, and a net.

5. In archery, you need a bow and _____.

6. A quarterback is someone who plays _____.

80

Sports Maze

Help the soccer player return to her team.

Sports Matching

Match the sport on the left to the correct equipment on the right. The first one has been done for you.

1. tennis   a. puck

2. gymnastics   b. helmet

3. croquet   c. running shoes

4. bicycling   d. racquet

5. track and field   e. parallel bars

6. hockey   f. mallet

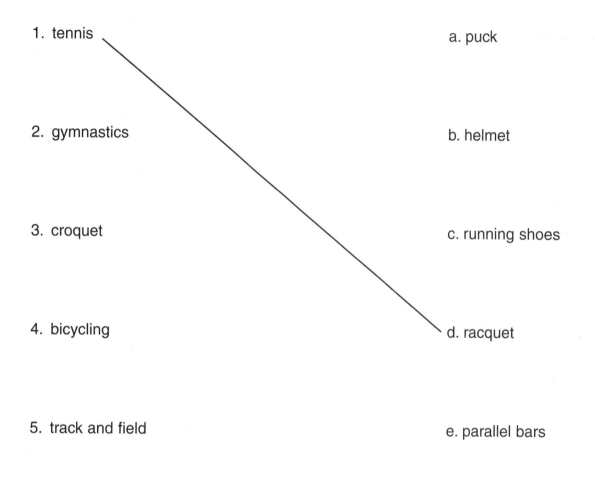

Sports Matching II

Match the sport on the left with the appropriate area on the right. The first one has been done for you.

1. beach volleyball

2. diving

3. snowshoeing

4. ice skating

5. golf

6. rock climbing

a. snow

b. mountain

c. sand

d. green

e. pool

f. rink

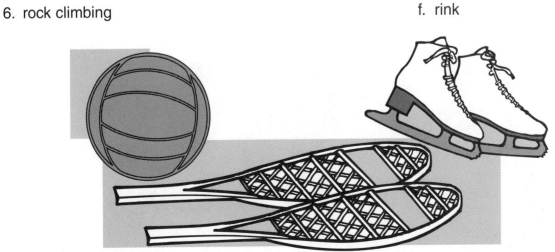

Sports Matching III

Match the sport on the left to the appropriate phrase on the right. The first one has been done for you.

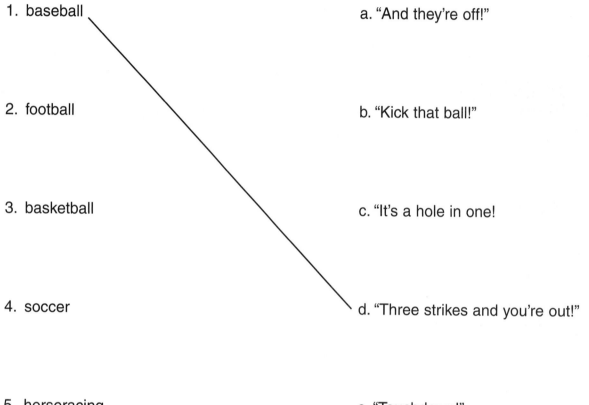

1. baseball

2. football

3. basketball

4. soccer

5. horseracing

6. golf

a. "And they're off!"

b. "Kick that ball!"

c. "It's a hole in one!

d. "Three strikes and you're out!"

e. "Touchdown!"

f. "Slam dunk!"

Sports Plates

Study each license plate for a clue to what sport its owner enjoys. The first one has been done for you.

1.    running

2.    _____

3.    _____

4.    _____

5.    _____

6.    _____

Favorite Sports

A Physical Education class took a survey on each student's favorite sport. Their choices were:

basketball	**baseball**
football	**swimming**

Sports	Tally	Number
	⊞⊞ I	
	⊞⊞ ⊞⊞ II	
	⊞⊞ ⊞⊞ I	
	⊞⊞ II	

The chart above shows the results of the survey, but doesn't include the sports. Using the clues below, fill in the name of each sport, and the total number of students who chose it as their favorite.

Clues:

- football was least popular
- baseball was chosen the most
- swimming got more votes than basketball

Answer Key

Page 5

2. He's painting the town red.

3. She's opening a can of worms.

4. They're crying over spilt milk.

5. She's pulling the wool over his eyes.

6. He's got a clean slate.

Page 6

2. She's showing him the ropes.

3. Bite your tongue!

4. He's dropping her a line.

5. He takes his hat off to him.

6. He's putting the cart before the horse.

Page 7

2. He's giving her a hand.

3. She's hitting the sack.

4. They let sleeping dogs lie.

5. She's pulling his leg.

6. He's catching some Zs.

Page 8

2. eye

3. mom

4. noon

5. nun

6. pop

Page 9

2. dad (or pop)

3. solo

4. wow

5. did

6. pup

Page 10

2. gig

3. bib

4. gag

5. kayak

6. Bob

Page 11

2. cds, records, tapes, etc.; these pieces make up a whole.

3. skin; these are protective coverings.

4. petals; these pieces make up a whole.

5. heat; these are the jobs of these appliances.

6. noodles; these parts make up a whole.

Page 12

2. head; these are protective or decorative coverings.

3. coins; these are pieces that go inside a container.

4. foot; these are parts of the body used in sports.

5. scales; these are protective coverings.

6. wheel; these allow movement

Page 13

2. leaf; these parts make up a whole.

3. toothbrush; these help in grooming body parts.

4. rake, broom, shovel, etc.; these are tools.

5. paintbrush, camera, clay, etc.; these are tools.

6. pool, lake, etc.; these are places in which to practice a skill.

Answer Key *(cont.)*

Page 14

2. band

3. arms

4. a. ease

   b. case

Page 15

2. a. croon

   b. crown

3. a. morn

   b. more

4. a. corns

   b. cores

Page 16

1. a. breed

   b. bread

2. a. floor

   b. flood

3. a. slap

   b. swap

4. a. more

   b. mole

Page 17

2. bark up the wrong tree

3. cry over spilt milk

4. rain on the parade

5. walk in the park

6. cat in the hat

Page 18

2. You deserve a break today.

3. big bad wolf

4. over the hill

5. feeling on top of the world

6. cross-country

Page 19

2. two eggs over easy

3. coffee break

4. close shave

5. slow down

6. who's on first

Page 20

2. blue goo

3. a grape ape

4. a dime lime

5. a fat rat

6. a groovy movie

Page 21

2. a happy pappy or glad dad

3. a lazy daisy

4. a mare hair

5. a fake snake

6. a calm Mom

Page 22

2. a funny bunny

3. a wee tree

4. a bug hug

5. an ink drink

6. a bird word

Answer Key *(cont.)*

Page 23

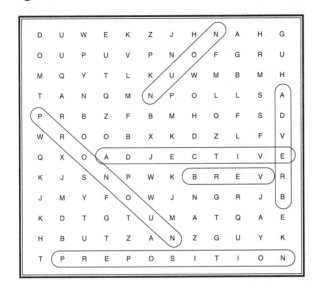

Page 24

2. aunt

3. son or daughter

4. uncle

5. grandmother

6. father or grandfather

Page 25

Answers will vary. The final answer should be the month, day, and year of the student's birthday.

Page 26

4	3	8
9	5	1
2	7	6

Page 27

A=14,196

E=22,897

H=22,926

M=17,829

R=39,790

L=22,757

G=18,642

W=39,416

N=18,784

Y=38,889

P=9,843

B=25,944

C=41,715

Z=17,901

F=16,864

J=29,601

T=29,424

D=52,584

X=28,455

O=33,804

K=16,325

S=50,124

I=54,776

1. OWL

2. BATS

3. WOLF

4. LYNX

5. WHALES

Answer Key (cont.)

Page 28

A=12	J=21	S=20
B=4	K=10	T=14
C=8	L=19	U=25
D=3	M=1	V=24
E=7	N=18	W=23
F=6	O=21	X=22
G=11	P=29	Y=28
H=5	Q=16	Z=31
I=2	R=13	

1. PLASTIC
2. POTATO
3. T.V.
4. SHORT
5. LEAK
6. NEWSPAPER

Page 29

D=5/8	O=4/5
R=1	P=0
W=3/5	C=7/8
A=1/2	T 3/10
N=1/3	U=5/6
F=1/6	J=2/7
G=2/5	V= 3
H=2/3	E=4
I=1/5	
K=7/15	
Y 2/7	
L=7/9	
M=1/7	
B=4/9	

1. LITTLE WOMEN
2. HARRY POTTER
3. JACK LONDON
4. DIARY
5. CARNIVAL

Page 30

	1	8	
7	5	2	4
	3	6	

Page 31

Page 32

Month	Rat's Name
January	
February	Whitey
March	Fluffy
April	
May	
June	Pinky
July	
August	
September	Sam and Annie
October	
November	Tiny
December	Templeton

Answer Key (cont.)

Page 33

```
R N T H Z D C Q Y E A E I R
B S C Y H W E L N V S T W F
R R A U P H P C S E F K R R
V I R X E I S T I R G Z D A
E A T Y T N O G C M M P I T
A T B L W U P F E B A P V C
D R U M R E O G I Z Y L I A
Q M S F R A C T I O N S D K
Z W E O Z T F T U H Y D E N
S D Y I B V R U Y T N W F V
V M U X K M C G Y O Y Y H N
M F D D K L T R P O N F U X
U T R D Y Z Z I B Z I N F K
O L Q S E L S U G N L T G E
```

Page 34

2. Ernie
3. Minnie Mouse
4. the Beast
5. Jill
6. the Hare

Page 35

2. The Three Bears
3. The Three Little Pigs
4. The Three Blind Mice
5. *Nina*, *Pinta*, and *Santa Maria*
6. Huey, Dewey, and Louie

Page 36

2. Andrew
3. Martin
4. Abraham
5. Jimmy
6. William

page 37

2. Rosa
3. Maya
4. Harriet
5. Emily
6. Christa

Page 38

2. lake
3. mountain
4. valley
4. hill
5. ocean
6. river

Page 39

2. volcano
3. desert
4. island
5. stream
6. waterfall

Page 40

How many people	How they traveled	Order in which they arrived
Two men	horseback	1
Family of four	horseback	2
Family of five	Covered wagon	3
Two couples	Covered wagon	4

Answer Key (cont.)

Page 41

2. bald eagle

3. Statue of Liberty

4. Stars and Stripes Forever

5. You're a Grand Old Flag

6. patriot

Page 42

2. free me

3. map chap

4. law flaw

5. flag bag

6. history mystery

Page 43

1. c

2. d

3. e

4. f

5. a

6. b

Page 44

1. d

2. c

3. a

4. b

5. f

6. e

Page 45

1. She's got guts.

2. I get a kick out of you.

3. He's so laid-back.

4. Stop making waves.

5. Don't sweat it.

6. It's a piece of cake.

Page 46

2. first ladies

3. famous monuments

4. official symbols of the U.S.

5. patriotic songs

6. U.S. money

Page 47

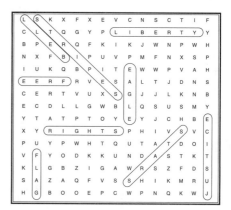

Page 48

2. Theodore Roosevelt

3. Mary Todd Lincoln

4. Martin Luther King, Jr.

5. Jimmy Carter

6. Betsy Ross

Page 49

1. chalk

2. homework

3. learn

4. apple

5. books

6. globe

Answer Key *(cont.)*

Page 50

2. ships

3. kayaks

4. airplane

5. automobile

6. bus

Page 51

Answers will vary according to year.

Page 52

Page 53

2. rocks (geology)

3. cats (veterinary medicine)

4. bones (paleontology)

5. birds (ornithology)

6. dogs (veterinary medicine)

Page 54

2. These are parts of the foot.

3. These are parts of the face.

4. These are parts of the mouth.

5. These are parts of the eye.

6. These are parts of the leg.

Page 55

1. d   4. f

2. e   5. c

3. b   6. a

Page 56

2. earring

3. body

4. elbow

5. toenail

6. pants

Page 57

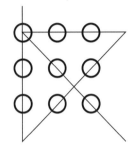

Page 58

2. radio

3. clock

4. oven

5. bike

6. television

Page 59

2. train

3. plane

4. boat

5. jet

6. skates

Page 60

2. telephone

3. X-ray

4. computer

5. microwave

6. microscope

Answer Key *(cont.)*

Page 61

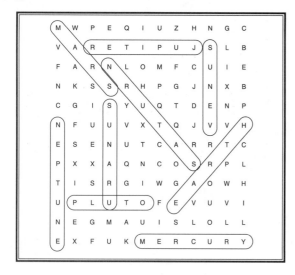

Page 62

1. a bouquet of pheasants
2. a watch of nightingales
3. a flight of swallows
4. a party of jays
5. a knot of hawks

Page 63

1. a run of salmon
2. a band of gorillas
3. a nest of caterpillars
4. a bed of clams
5. a school of fish
6. a leap of leopards

Page 64

Position in parade	Number of students	Costume
1	4	beetles
2	3	spiders
3	10	centipedes
4	6	ants
5	1	frog

Page 65

Move the penny at the right in the top row and the penny of the bottom rowpenny at the bottom between the two rows of pennies

Page 66

The pattern is vowel-consonant-vowel, or consonant-vowel-consonant.

Page 67

Page 68

2. 4 paws on a cat
3. 1 wheel on a unicycle
4. 12 numbers on a clock
5. 8 sides on a stop sign
6. 8 legs on a spider

Page 69

2. 7 continents in the world
3. 32 teeth in your mouth
4. 7 days in a week
5. 24 hours in a day
6. ten fingers on your hands

Page 70

1. soccer
2. polo
3. baseball or softball
4. fencing
5. boxing
6. dogsledding

Answer Key *(cont.)*

Page 71

1. bases
2. puck
3. helmet
4. racquet
5. mallet
6. paddles

Page 72

2. Category: Parts of a bicycle
3. Category: Places on which people play sports.
4. Category: Protective gear.
5. Category: Items you ride in or on while playing sports.
6. Category: Sports footwear.

Page 73

2. Category: Equipment that is hit by an object.
3. Category: Places in which to play sports.
4. Category: Clothing in which to play sports.
5. Category: Sports footwear.
6. Category: Protective gear for your head.

Page 74

Hiking Spots	Tally	Number
Beach	||||| ||||| ||	12
Lake	||||	4
Mountains	|||	3
River	|||||	5

Page 75

red, yellow,
red, yellow, blue,
red, yellow, blue, green,
red, yellow, blue, green, pink,
red, yellow, blue, green, pink, orange,
red, yellow, blue, green, pink, orange, purple,
red, yellow, blue, green, pink, orange, purple, white

Total Stripes: = 35

Page 76

1/2 mile run, 1 mile jog; 1 mile run, 2 mile jog.

Page 77

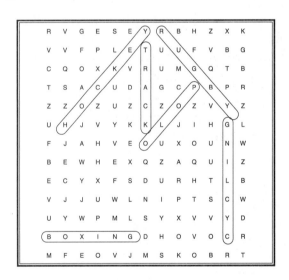

Page 78

2. hoop
3. batter
4. wheels
5. soccer
6. ball

Answer Key *(cont.)*

Page 79

2. pool

3. tennis

4. runners/joggers

5. food

6. skiing

Page 80

2. knee pads

3. wheels

4. volleyball

5. arrow

6. football

Page 81

Page 82

1. d

2. e

3. f

4. b

5. c

6. a

Page 83

1. c

2. e

3. a

4. f

5. d

6. b

Page 84

1. d

2. e

3. f

4. b

5. a

6. c

Page 85

2. tennis

3. golf

4. swimming

5. cycling

6. ping pong

Page 86

Sports	Tally	Number
football	ᵀᴴᴸ I	6
baseball	ᵀᴴᴸ ᵀᴴᴸ II	12
swimming	ᵀᴴᴸ ᵀᴴᴸ I	11
basketball	ᵀᴴᴸ II	7